C

Baby Bootie
Boutique

An Annie Original

Little Red Sandals

READ BEFORE STARTING

Some of the rnds in this set may not always end or begin where you think they should, but follow the directions as they are written to put the shaping on the booties in just the right places.

SIZES:
Small Sole is 3½" long. Medium Sole is 4¼" long. Large Sole is 5" long.

MATERIALS:
❑ Worsted yarn:
38 yds. white
23 yds. red
18 yds. brown
❑ F or G hook or hook needed to obtain gauge

GAUGES:
F hook, 9 sc = 2"; 9 sc rows = 2".
G hook, 4 sc = 1"; 4 sc rows = 1".

BASIC STITCHES:
Ch, sl st, sc, hdc, dc.

NOTES:
Do not join rnds unless otherwise stated.
For **Small,** use F hook and directions outside brackets [ ].
For **Medium,** use G hook and directions outside brackets [ ].
For **Large,** use G hook and directions inside brackets [ ].

SOLE & SIDE
Rnd 1: With brown, ch 12 [14], sc in second ch from hook, sc in next 7 [9] chs, hdc in next ch, 2 hdc in next ch, 5 hdc in end ch; working in remaining lps on opposite side

of starting ch, 2 hdc in next ch, hdc in next ch, sc in next 7 [9] chs, 2 sc in next ch.

Rnd 2: 2 sc in next st, sc in next 10 [12] sts, (2 sc in next st, sc in next st) 3 times, sc in next 9 [11] sts, 2 sc in next st, sc in next st.

Rnd 3: 2 sc in next st, sc in next 11 [13] sts, (2 sc in next st, sc in next st) 2 times, (sc in next st, 2 sc in next st) 2 times, sc in next 11 [13] sts, 2 sc in next st, sc in next st, join with sl st in next st. Fasten off.

Rnd 4: For **Side,** working in **back lps** only *(see Stitch Guide),* join red with sc in the st before sl st of last rnd, sc in each sc around. *(39 sc made) [43 sc made]*

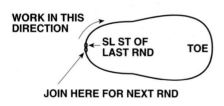

WORK IN THIS DIRECTION

SL ST OF LAST RND

TOE

JOIN HERE FOR NEXT RND

Rnd 5: Sc in each st around.

Rnd 6: Sc in next 13 [15] sts, (skip next st, sc in next 2 sts) 4 times, sc in next 14 [16 sts].

Rnd 7: Sc in next 12 [14] sts, (skip next st, sc in next st) 5 times, sc in next 13 [15] sts, join with sl st in **back lp** of next st. Fasten off. *(30 sc) [34 sc]*

STOCKING

Row 1: Join white with sc in **back lp** of sc just before sl st of last rnd

on Side, sc in next 12 [14] sts, skip next st, sc in next 3 sts, skip next st, sl st in next st, turn.

NOTE: *In the next several rows, you will be working back and forth across the toe end of shoe to form instep. When working into the red sts, work in **back lps** only; when you turn and are working in the white sts made at toe, work in both lps.*

Row 2: Skip sl st, sc in next 3 sts, skip next st on white side, sl st in next st, turn.

Row 3: Skip sl st, sc in next 3 sts, sl st in **back lp** of next st on red side, turn.

Row 4: Skip sl st, sc in next 3 sts, skip next st on white side, sl st in next st, turn.

Row 5: Skip sl st, sc in next 3 sts, sc in **back lps** of next 10 [12] sts on red side.

Rnd 6: For **Small and Medium** only, sc in next 22 sts.

Rnd [6]: For **Large** only, sc in next 10 sts, skip next st, sc in next 3 sts, skip next st, sc in next 11 sts.

Rnds 7–8: For all sizes, sc in next 22 [24] sts.

Rnd 9: Ch 3, dc in each st around, join with sl st in top of ch-3. *(22 dc) [24 dc]*

Rnds 10–11: Ch 3, **dc front post** *(dc fp—see Stitch Guide)* around next st, dc fp around each st of rnd, join. For **Small and Medium** only, fasten off at end of rnd 11.

Rnd [12]: For **Large** only, ch 3, dc fp around each st of rnd, join. Fasten off.

STRAPS
Center Strap
Row 1: Working in remaining **front lps** of the center 2 sts on rnd 7 of Side at toe end of shoe, join red with sc in first st, sc in last st, turn. *(2 sc made)*

Row 2: Skip first st, sc in last st, turn. *(1 sc)*

Rows 3–5: Ch 1, sc in st, turn.

Row 6: Ch 1, sc in st, ch 4, turn; sl st in **back bar** *(see illustration)* of first sc on row 2, forming a loop behind Strap just made. Fasten off.

BACK BAR

Side Straps
For first **Side Strap,** working in remaining **front lps** of rnd 7 on Side, join red with sl st in third st to the right of Center Strap; working behind Center Strap, ch 6, sl st in corresponding st on opposite side of shoe. Fasten off.

For second **Side Strap,** skip 2 sts to right of first Side Strap, join red with sl st in next st, ch 8; leaving an 8" end, cut yarn, drop lp from hook; thread ch-8 through loop behind Center Strap, replace lp on hook and sl st in corresponding st on opposite side of shoe. Fasten off.

EDGE OF SOLE
Hold Sole pointing away from you; working in remaining **front lps** of rnd 3 on Sole, join brown with sl st, sl st loosely in each st around. Fasten off. ❏❏

High Top Tennis

SIZES:
Small Sole is 3½" long.
Medium Sole is 4¼" long.
Large Sole is 5" long.

MATERIALS:
- Worsted yarn:
  - 35 yds. white
  - 6 yds. red
  - 45 yds. black
- Tapestry needle
- F or G hook or hook needed to obtain gauge

GAUGES:
F hook, 9 sc = 2"; 9 sc rows = 2".
G hook, 4 sc = 1"; 4 sc rows = 1".

BASIC STITCHES:
Ch, sl st, sc, hdc, dc.

NOTES:
Do not join rnds unless otherwise stated.

For **Small,** use F hook and directions outside brackets [ ].

For **Medium,** use G hook and directions outside brackets [ ].

For **Large,** use G hook and directions inside brackets [ ].

SOLE
Rnd 1: With white, ch 12 [14], sc in second ch from hook, sc in next 7 [9] chs, hdc in next ch, 2 hdc in next ch, 5 hdc in end ch; working in remaining lps on opposite side of starting ch, 2 hdc in next ch, hdc in next ch, sc in next 7 [9] chs, 2 sc in next ch.

Rnd 2: 2 sc in next st, sc in next 10 [12] sts, (2 sc in next st, sc in next st) 3 times, sc in next 9 [11] sts, 2 sc in next st, sc in next st.

Rnd 3: 2 sc in next st, sc in next 11 [13] sts, (2 sc in next st, sc in next st) 2 times, (sc in next st, 2 sc in next st) 2 times, sc in next 11 [13] sts, 2 sc in next st, sc in next st, join with sl st in next st, **turn.**

Rnd 4: For **Edge of Sole,** working in **back lps** only *(see Stitch Guide),* ch 1, sc in each sc around, join with sl st in first sc. Fasten off. *(39 sc made) [43 sc made]*

Rnd 5: With Edge of Sole facing you, working in remaining **front lps** of rnd 3, join red with sc in first st after sl st of rnd 3, sc in each st around, join with sl st in first sc. Fasten off.

Rnd 6: Join white with sc in same st as last sl st, sc in next 14 [16] sts, skip next st, dc in next 2 sts, dc next 2 sts tog, dc in next 2 sts, skip next st, sc in next 16 [18] sts, join. Fasten off.

TONGUE
Row 1: Working in **back lps** only of center 7 sts of last rnd at toe end of Sole, join black with sc in first st, sc in next 6 sts, turn. *(7 sc made)*

Rows 2–4: Ch 1, sc in each st across, turn.

Rows 5–6: Ch 1, skip first st, sc in each st across, turn. *(6 sc, 5 sc)*

Rows 7–8: Ch 1, sc in each st across, turn.

Row 9: Ch 1, skip first st, sc in each st across, turn. *(4 sc)*

Rows 10–13: Ch 1, sc in each st across, turn. At end of last row, fasten off.

SIDE

Row 1: Working in **back lps** only of rnd 6 on Sole, join black with sc in first st after row 1 on Tongue, sc in each st across to corresponding st at beginning of row 1 on Tongue, turn. *(29 sc made) [33 sc made]*

Row 2 Ch 1, sc in each st across, turn.

Row 3: Ch 1, skip first st, sc in next 26 [30] sts, sc last 2 sts tog, turn.

Row 4: Ch 1, skip first st, sc in next st, sc next 2 sts tog, sc in next 19 [23] sts, (sc next 2 sts tog) 2 times, turn.

Row 5: Ch 1, skip first st, sc in next 20 [24] sts, sc last 2 sts tog, turn.

Row 6: Ch 1, skip first st, sc in next 18 [22] sts, sc last 2 sts tog, turn.

Rows 7–10: Ch 1, sc in each st across, turn. At end of last row, fasten off.

TRIM

Join white with sc in first st of last row on Side, sc in each st across *(do not crochet in top edge of Tongue)*. Fasten off.

SHOESTRING

With white, ch 110. Fasten off.

Lace Shoestring through edges of Side as shown in photo. Tie ends in a bow.

CIRCLE (Make 2 for each shoe)

With white, ch 2, 6 sc in second ch from hook, join with sl st in first sc. Leaving long end for sewing, fasten off.

Sew one Circle to each side of Shoe *(see photo).* ❑❑

Mary Jane Shoes

SIZES:
Small Sole is 3½" long.
Medium Sole is 4¼" long.
Large Sole is 5" long.

MATERIALS:
❏ Worsted yarn:
  35 yds. black
  39 yds. white
❏ F or G hook or hook needed to obtain gauge

GAUGES:
F hook, 9 sc = 2"; 9 sc rows = 2".
G hook, 4 sc = 1"; 4 sc rows = 1".

BASIC STITCHES:
Ch, sl st, sc, hdc, dc.

NOTES:
Do not join rnds unless otherwise stated.
For **Small,** use F hook and directions outside brackets [ ].
For **Medium,** use G hook and directions outside brackets [ ].
For **Large,** use G hook and directions inside brackets [ ].

SOLE & SIDE
Rnd 1: With black, ch 12 [14], sc in second ch from hook, sc in next 7 [9] chs, hdc in next ch, 2 hdc in next ch, 5 hdc in end ch; working in remaining lps on opposite side of starting ch, 2 hdc in next ch, hdc in next ch, sc in next 7 [9] chs, 2 sc in next ch.

Rnd 2: 2 sc in next st, sc in next 10 [12] sts, (2 sc in next st, sc in next st) 3 times, sc in next 9 [11] sts, 2 sc in next st, sc in next st.

Rnd 3: 2 sc in next st, sc in next 11 [13] sts, (2 sc in next st, sc in next st) 2 times, (sc in next st, 2 sc in next st) 2 times, sc in next 11 [13] sts, 2 sc in next st, sc in next st, join with sl st in next st.

Rnd 4: For **Side,** working in **back lps** only *(see Stitch Guide),* sc in each sc around. *(39 sc made)* [43 sc made]

Rnd 5: Sc in each sc around.

Rnd 6: Sc in next 14 [16] sts, (skip next st, sc in next 2 sts) 4 times, sc next 13 [15] sts.

Rnd 7: Sc in next 13 [15] sts, (skip next st, sc in next st) 5 times, sc in next 12 [14] sts, join with sl st in **back lp** of first sc of rnd. Fasten off. *(30 sc)* [34 sc]

STOCKING
Row 1: Join white with sc in **back lp** of st before sl st of last rnd on Side, sc in next 13 [14] sts, skip next st, sc in next 3 sts, skip next st, sl st in next, turn.

NOTE: *In the next several rows, you will be working back and forth across the toe end of shoe to form instep. When working into the black sts, work in **back lps** only; when you turn and are working in the white sts made at toe, work in both lps.*

Row 2: Skip sl st, sc in next 3 sts, skip next st on white side, sl st in next st, turn.

Row 3: Skip sl st, sc in next 3 sts, skip next st on black side, sl st in **back lp** of next st, turn.

Row 4: Skip sl st, sc in next 3 sts, skip next st on white side, sl st in next st, turn.

Row 5: Skip sl st, sc in next 3 sts, skip next st on black side, sc in **back lps** of next 7 [10] sts.

Rnd 6: For **Small and Medium** only, sc in next 20 sts.

Rnd [6]: For **Large** only, sc in next 10 sts, skip next st, sc in next 3 sts, skip next st, sc in next 9 sts.

Rnds 7–9: For all sizes, sc in next 20 [22] sts. At end of last rnd, join with sl st in first sc.

Rnd 10: Working in **back lps** only, ch 3, dc in each st around, join with sl st in top of ch-3. *(20 dc) [22 dc]*

Rnds 11–12: Ch 3, **dc front post** *(dc fp—see Stitch Guide)* around next st, dc fp around each st of rnd, join. For **Small and Medium** only, fasten off at end of rnd 12.

Rnd [13]: For **Large** only, ch 3, dc fp around each st of rnd, join. Fasten off.

TRIM
Working in **front lps** of rnd 9, join white with sc in first st, ch 2, (sc in next st, ch 2) around, join with sl st in first sc. Fasten off.

ANKLE STRAPS
Join black with sc to a **front lp** on outer edge of Side on one shoe, ch 8 [9], sl st in corresponding **front lp** on opposite edge of Side, ch 3, sl st in same st again. Fasten off.

For other shoe, join on opposite side to start. ❑❑

Cowboy Boots

SIZES:
Small Sole is 3½" long.
Medium Sole is 4¼" long.
Large Sole is 5" long.

MATERIALS:
❑ Worsted yarn:
  50 yds. brown
  40 yds. gold
❑ Tapestry needle
❑ F or G hook or hook needed to obtain gauge

GAUGES:
F hook, 9 sc = 2"; 9 sc rows = 2".
G hook, 4 sc = 1"; 4 sc rows = 1".

BASIC STITCHES:
Ch, sl st, sc, hdc, dc.

NOTES:
Do not join rnds unless otherwise stated.
For **Small,** use F hook and directions outside brackets [ ].
For **Medium,** use G hook and directions outside brackets [ ].
For **Large,** use G hook and directions inside brackets [ ].

SOLE
Rnd 1: With brown, ch 12 [14], sc in second ch from hook, sc in next 7 [9] chs, hdc in next ch, 2 hdc in next ch, 5 hdc in end ch; working in remaining lps on opposite side of starting ch, 2 hdc in next ch, hdc in next ch, sc

in next 7 [9] chs, 2 sc in next ch.
Rnd 2: 2 sc in next st, sc in next 10 [12] sts, (2 sc in next st, sc in next st) 3 times, sc in next 9 [11] sts, 2 sc in next st, sc in next st.
Rnd 3: 2 sc in next st, sc in next 11 [13] sts, (2 sc in next st, sc in next st) 2 times, (sc in next st, 2 sc in next st) 2 times, sc in next 11 [13] sts, 2 sc in next st, sc in next st, join with sl st in next st, **turn.**
Rnd 4: For **Edge of Sole,** working in **back lps** only *(see Stitch Guide),* ch 1, sc in each sc around, join with sl st in first sc. Fasten off. *(39 sc made)* [43 sc made]

SIDE
Row 1: *(This is a small section worked on middle 13 sts at heel.)* Working in **front lps** of rnd 3, join brown with sl st in first st of 13 sts around back of heel *(see illustration),* sc in next 11 sts, sl st in next st. Fasten off.

← JOIN WITH SL ST

Rnd 2: Working in sts of row 1 and in remaining **front lps** of rnd 3, join gold with sc in center st of row 1 at heel, sc in each st around. *(39 sc made) [43 sc made]*

Rnd 3: Sc in next 14 [16] sts, skip next st, hdc in next st, skip next st, dc in next 2 sts, dc next 2 sts tog, dc in next 2 sts, skip next st, hdc in next st, skip next st, sc in next 13 [15] sts.

Rnd 4: Sc in next 13 [15] sts, skip next st, sc in next st, skip next st, sc in next 3 sts, skip next st, sc in next st, skip next st, sc in next 12 [14] sts.

Rnd 5: Sc in next 12 [14] sts, (skip next st, sc in next st) 4 times, sc in next 10 [12] sts.

Rnd 6: Sc in next 6 [7] sts, sl st in next 5 [6] sts, skip next st, sc in next 3 sts, skip next st, sl st in next 5 [6] sts, sc in next 5 [6] sts, sc in first st of rnd, join with sl st in next. Fasten off.

Rnd 7: Working in **back lps** only, join brown with sc in st before joining sl st of last rnd, sc in next 10 [12] sts, skip next st, sc in next 2 sts, skip next st, sc in next 9 [11] sts.

Rnd 8: For **Small and Medium** only, sc in next 22 sts.

Rnd [8]: For **Large** only, sc in next 12 sts, skip next st, sc in next 2 sts, skip next st, sc in next 10 sts. *[24 sc]*

Rnds 9–10: Sc in each st around.

Rnd 11: 2 sc in next st, sc in next 11 [12] sts, 2 sc in next st, sc in next 9 [10] sts, sc in first st of rnd. *(24 sc) [26 sc]*

Rnds 12–14: Sc in each st around.

Rnd 15: Sc in next 4 [5] sts, hdc in next st, skip next st, dc in next st, 4 dc in next st, dc in next st, skip next st, hdc in next st, sc in next 5 [6] sts, hdc in next st, skip next st, dc in next st, 4 dc in next st, dc in next st, skip next st, hdc in next st, sc in next st, join with sl st in first sc of rnd. Fasten off.

TOP EDGE

Rnd 1: Join gold with sc in center back st on last rnd of Side, sc in each st around with 2 sc in the second dc of each 4-dc group.

Rnd 2: Skip first st, sc in each st around with 2 sc in the second sc of each 2-sc group, join with sl st in first sc. Fasten off.

FRONT DECORATION

Row 1: Working in the center front 3 remaining **front lps** of rnd 6 on Side, join gold in first st, sc in each of next 2 sts, turn. *(3 sc made)*

Rows 2–3: Ch 1, sc in each st across, turn.

Row 4: Ch 1, (sc, hdc) in first st, 3 dc in next st, (hdc, sc) in last st. Fasten off.

Tack top edge of Decoration in

place on front of Side *(see photo).*

SIDE DECORATION
(make 2 for each Boot)
With gold, ch 25 [30]. Fasten off. Arrange one Decoration piece in a loop design on each side of Boot *(see illustration)* and tack in place. ❑❑

Sandals

SIZES:
Small Sole is 3½" long.
Medium Sole is 4¼" long.
Large Sole is 5" long.

MATERIALS:
❑ Worsted yarn:
  25 yds. tan
  25 yds. white
❑ 2 small white shank buttons
❑ Tapestry needle
❑ F or G hook or hook needed to obtain gauge

GAUGES:
F hook, 9 sc = 2"; 9 sc rows = 2".
G hook, 4 sc = 1"; 4 sc rows = 1".

BASIC STITCHES:
Ch, sl st, sc, hdc, dc.

NOTES:
Do not join rnds unless otherwise stated.
For **Small,** use F hook and directions outside brackets [ ].
For **Medium,** use G hook and directions outside brackets [ ]. For **Large,** use G hook and directions inside brackets [ ].

SOLE
Rnd 1: With tan, ch 12 [14], sc in second ch from hook, sc in next 7 [9] chs, hdc in next ch, 2 hdc in next ch, 5 hdc in end ch; working in remaining lps on opposite side of starting ch, 2 hdc in next ch, hdc in next ch, sc in next 7 [9] chs, 2 sc in next ch.

Rnd 2: 2 sc in next st, sc in next 10 [12] sts, (2 sc in next st, sc in next st) 3 times, sc in next 9 [11] sts, 2 sc in next st, sc in next st.

Rnd 3: 2 sc in next st, sc in next 11 [13] sts, (2 sc in next st, sc in next st) 2 times, (sc in next st, 2 sc in next st) 2 times, sc in next 11 [13] sts, 2 sc in next st, sc in next st, join with sl st in next st, **turn.**

Rnd 4: For **Edge of Sole,** working in **back lps** only *(see Stitch Guide),* ch 1, sc in each sc around, join with sl st in first sc. Fasten off.

(39 sc made) [43 sc made]

TOE
First Side
Row 1: Mark the center 6 sts of rnd 3 at toe end of Sole; with bottom of Sole facing you, count 9 sts past marked sts *(see illustration)*; working in remaining **front lps,** join white with sl st in ninth st; working toward toe end, ch 3, dc in next 3 sts, skip next st, dc in next 4 sts, turn.

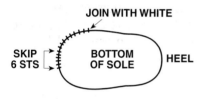

JOIN WITH WHITE

SKIP 6 STS

BOTTOM OF SOLE

HEEL

Row 2: Ch 3, dc in next 2 sts, skip next st, dc in next 3 sts, skip last st, turn.

Row 3: Skip first st, sc in next 2 sts, skip next st, sc in next st, skip last st. Fasten off.

Second Side
Row 1: Skip the 6 marked sts at toe end; with bottom of Sole facing away from you and toe end pointing to the left, count 9 sts past marked sts, join white with sl st in ninth st; working toward toe end, ch 3, dc in next 3 sts, skip next st, dc in next 4 sts, turn.

Row 2: Ch 3, dc in next 2 sts, skip next st, dc in next 3 sts, skip

last st, turn.

Row 3: Skip first st, sc in next 2 sts, skip next st, sc in next st, skip last st, turn.

Row 4: Match sts of row 3 on First and Second Sides together; working through both thicknesses, sc in each st across, forming top seam.

Row 5: With toe end of Sole pointing down, sc in edge of Side just to the right of top seam *(see illustration at right),* skip seam, sc in edge of Side just to the left of top seam, turn. *(2 sc)*

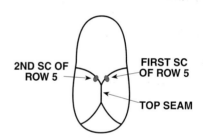

2ND SC OF ROW 5

FIRST SC OF ROW 5

TOP SEAM

Rows 6–11: Ch 1, sc in each st across, turn. At end of last row, leaving a long end for sewing, fasten off.

Fold rows 6–11 in half, forming a loop at end of top seam *(see illustration).* Sew last row to back of row 6.

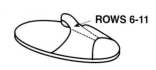

ROWS 6-11

BACK

Row 1: With white, ch 4 [6]; working in the center 7 sts at heel end of Sole, dc in each of 7 sts, ch 5 [7], turn.

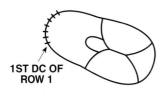

1ST DC OF ROW 1

Row 2: Sc in second ch from hook, sc in next 3 [5] chs, sc in next 7 sts, sc in next 4 [6] chs, turn.

Row 3: Ch 1, sc in each st across.

For **Front Strap on first Sandal,** ch 12, sc in fifth ch from hook, ch 2, skip next 2 chs, sc in next ch, ch 4, join with sl st in end of row 2. Fasten off.

For **Front Strap on second Sandal,** fasten off at end of row 3; join white with sl st in first sc at beginning of row 3, ch 12, sc in fifth ch from hook, ch 2, skip next 2 chs, sc in next ch, ch 4, join with sl st in end of row 2. Fasten off.

Thread Strap through loop at top of Toe. Sew button to ends of rows 1 and 2 on Back opposite from Strap. ❑❑

Granny Boots

SIZES:
Small Sole is 3½" long.
Medium Sole is 4¼" long.
Large Sole is 5" long.

MATERIALS:
❏ Worsted yarn:
   20 yds. lt. blue
   25 yds. med. blue
   6 yds. dk. blue
   20 yds. gold
   10 yds. off-white
   10 yds. green
   12 yds. lt. pink
   3 yds. bright pink
❏ Tapestry needle
❏ F or G hook or hook needed
   to obtain gauge

GAUGES:
F hook, 9 sc = 2"; 9 sc rows = 2".
G hook, 4 sc = 1"; 4 sc rows = 1".

BASIC STITCHES:
Ch, sl st, sc, hdc, dc.

NOTES:
Do not join rnds unless other-wise stated.
For **Small,** use F hook and directions outside brackets [ ].
For **Medium,** use G hook and directions outside brackets [ ].
For **Large,** use G hook and directions inside brackets [ ].

SOLE, SIDE & TOP
Rnd 1: With med. blue, ch 12 [14], sc in second ch from hook, sc in next 7 [9] chs, hdc in next ch, 2 hdc in next ch, 5 hdc in end ch; working in remaining lps on opposite side of starting ch, 2 hdc in next ch, hdc in next ch, sc in next 7 [9] chs, 2 sc in next ch.

Rnd 2: 2 sc in next st, sc in next 10 [12] sts, (2 sc in next st, sc in next st) 3 times, sc in next 9 [11] sts, 2 sc in next st, sc in next st.

Rnd 3: 2 sc in next st, sc in next 11 [13] sts, (2 sc in next st, sc in next st) 2 times, (sc in next st, 2 sc in next st) 2 times, sc in next 11 [13] sts, 2 sc in next st, sc in next st, join with sl st in next st.

Rnd 4: For **Side,** working in **back lps** only *(see Stitch Guide),* sc in each sc around. *(39 sc made) [43 sc made]*

Rnd 5: Sc in next 13 [15] sts, skip next st, hdc in next st, skip next st, dc in next 2 sts, dc next 2 sts tog, dc in next 2 sts, skip next st, hdc in next st, skip next st, sc in next 14 [16] sts, join with sl st in next st. Fasten off.

Rnd 6: Working in **back lps** only, join lt. pink with sc in st before last sl st, sc in next 12 [14] sts, skip next st, sc in next st, skip next st, sc in next 3 sts, skip next st, sc in next st, skip next st, sc in next 12 [14] sts.

Rnd 7: Sc in next 12 [14] sts, (skip next st, sc in next st) 4 times, sc in next 10 [12] sts, join with sl st in next st. Fasten off.

Rnd 8: Join gold with sc in same st as sl st, sc in next 10 [12] sts, skip next st, sc in next 3 sts, skip next st, sc in next 10 [12] sts.

Rnd 9: Sc in next 11 [13] sts, skip next st, sc in next 2 sts, skip next st, sc in next 9 [11] sts, join with sl st in next st. Fasten off.

NOTES: *The decorative embroidery will be worked on the piece as you work remaining rnds of the piece.*

For **long dc,** *yo, insert hook into top of st on row before last, yo, pull up a long lp (see illustration), (yo, pull through 2 lps on hook) 2 times.*

With lt. blue, overcast *(see illustration)* each **front lp** of rnd 5.

OVERCAST

With dk. blue, using straight stitch *(see illustration)*, embroider small V stitches evenly spaced on lt. pink rnds.

STRAIGHT STITCH

Rnd 10: For **Top,** join lt. blue with sc in same st as sl st on last rnd, ***long dc** (see Notes)* in next st on rnd before last, sc in next st on last rnd; repeat from * around, join with sl st in first sc. Fasten off.

Rnd 11: Join off-white with sc in same st as last sl st, sc in each st around. *(22 sc) [26 sc]*

Rnds 12–13: Sc in each st around. At end of last rnd, join with sl st in first sc. Fasten off.

NOTES: *For **3-dc cluster,** yo, insert hook in st, yo, pull through st, yo, pull through 2 lps on hook, (yo, insert hook in same st, yo, pull through st, yo, pull through 2 lps on hook) 2 times, yo and pull through all 4 lps on hook.*

With gold yarn, using cross stitch *(see illustration)*, embroider X's evenly spaced around the center of white rnds.

CROSS STITCH

2 4
3 1

Rnd 14: Join green with sc in same st last sl st, **3-dc cluster** *(see Notes)* in next st, *sc in next st, 3-dc cluster in next st; repeat from * around, join with sl st in first sc. Fasten off.

Rnd 15: Join lt. blue with sc in same st as last sl st, sc in each st around.

Rnds 16–17: Sc in each st around. At end of last rnd, join with sl st in first sc. Fasten off.

Rnd 18: Join gold with sc in same st as last sl st, 3-dc cluster in next st, (sc in next st, 3-dc cluster in next st) around, join. Fasten off.

Rnd 19: Join dk. blue with sc in same st as last sl st, sc in each st around, join with sl st in first sc. Fasten off.

With bright pink, embroider French knots *(see illustration)* evenly space around the center of lt. blue rnds. ❑❑

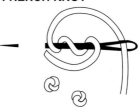

FRENCH KNOT

Roller Skates

SIZES:

Small Sole is 3½" long.
Medium Sole is 4¼" long.
Large Sole is 5" long.

MATERIALS:

❑ Worsted yarn:
   54 yds. white
   30 yds. gray
   20 yds. dk. brown
❑ 22 yds. pink baby yarn
❑ Polyester fiberfill
❑ Tapestry needle
❑ F or G hook or hook needed to obtain gauge

GAUGES:

F hook, 9 sc = 2"; 9 sc rows = 2".
G hook, 4 sc = 1"; 4 sc rows = 1".

BASIC STITCHES:

Ch, sl st, sc, hdc, dc.

NOTES:

Do not join rnds unless otherwise stated.

For **Small,** use F hook and directions outside brackets [ ].

For **Medium,** use G hook and directions outside brackets [ ].

For **Large,** use G hook and directions inside brackets [ ].

SOLE

Rnd 1: With dk. brown, ch 12 [14], sc in second ch from hook, sc in next 7 [9] chs, hdc in next ch, 2 hdc in next ch, 5 hdc in end ch; working in remaining lps on opposite side of starting ch, 2 hdc in next ch, hdc in next ch, sc in next 7 [9] chs, 2 sc in next ch.

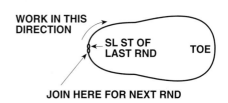

WORK IN THIS DIRECTION
SL ST OF LAST RND
TOE
JOIN HERE FOR NEXT RND

Rnd 2: 2 sc in next st, sc in next 10 [12] sts, (2 sc in next st, sc in next st) 3 times, sc in next 9 [11] sts, 2 sc in next st, sc in next st.

Rnd 3: 2 sc in next st, sc in next 11 [13] sts, (2 sc in next st, sc in next st) 2 times, (sc in next st, 2 sc in next st) 2 times, sc in next 11 [13] sts, 2 sc in next st, sc in next st, join with sl st in next st. Fasten off.

SIDE

Rnd 1: Working in **back lps** only *(see Stitch Guide)*, join white with sc in st before sl st of last rnd, sc in each sc around. *(39 sc made)* [43 sc made]

Rnd 2: Sc in each sc around.

Rnd 3: Sc in next 14 [18] sts, (skip next st, sc in next 2 sts) 3 times, skip next st, sc in next 15 [15] sts.

Rnd 4: Sc in next 13 [16] sts, (sc next 2 sts tog) 5 times, sc in next 12 [13] sts, join with sl st in next st. Fasten off.

TONGUE

Row 1: Working in **back lps** of center 5 sts at toe end of rnd 4 on Side of shoe, join white with sc in first st, sc in next 4 sts, turn. *(5 sc made)*

Row 2: Ch 1, skip first sc, sc in next 4 sts, turn.

Rows 3–14: Ch 1, sc in each st across, turn. At end of last row, fasten off.

TOP

Row 1: Starting at toe end of shoe, join white with sc in **front lp** of last st of 5 center sts; working in **both lps,** sc in next 25 [29] unworked sts of rnd 4 on Side, sc in **front lp** of first st of 5 center sts, turn. *(The remaining 3 center sts across front of toe should be left unworked.)*

JOIN

Row 2: Ch 1, skip first st, sc in next 24 [28] sts, skip next st, sc in last st, turn.

Row 3: Ch 1, skip first st, sc in next st, skip next st, sc in next 18 [22] sts, (skip next st, sc in next st) 2 times, turn.

Row 4: Ch 1, skip first st, sc in next 18 [22] sts, skip next st, sc in last st, turn.

Row 5: Ch 1, skip first st, sc in next 16 [20] sts, skip next st, sc in last st, turn.

Rows 6–11: Ch 1, sc in each st across, turn. At end of last row, fasten off. *(17 sc)* [21 sc]

SHOESTRING

With F hook and pink baby yarn, leaving a long end at beginning and end, ch 130. Fasten off.

Lace Shoestring up edges of Top at front of shoe.

POMPOM
(make 2 for each Slipper)
Using full-size pattern Piece *(see page 10)*, cut two rings from cardboard. Cut four 30" strands of pink baby yarn and wrap each around the two rings which have been placed together. Cut around outer edge between the two cardboard rings. Tie a separate strand of pink yarn tightly between the rings. Remove rings.

POM-POM PATTERN

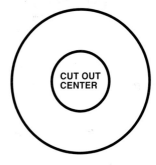

CUT OUT
CENTER

Using long end, tie each Pompom to each end of Shoestring at front of Shoe.

EDGE OF SOLE
Hold Sole pointing away from you; working in remaining **front lps** of rnd 3 on Sole, join dk. brown with sl st in first st, sl st loosely in each st around. Fasten off.

WHEEL (make 4 for each Shoe)
Rnd 1: With gray, ch 2, 6 sc in second ch from hook. *(6 sc made)*
Rnd 2: 2 sc in each st around, join with sl st in next st. *(12 sc)*
Rnd 3: Working in **back lps** only, sc in each st around.
Rnd 4: Working in **both lps,** sc in each st around.
Rnd 5: Sc in each st around, join with sl st in next st. Place a small amount of fiberfill inside Wheel.
Rnd 6: Working in **back lps** only, (skip next st, sc in next st) 5 times, skip next 2 sts, sl st in **both lps** of next st. Fasten off.
Evenly spacing Wheels apart at each end, tack Wheels to bottom of Sole. Tack inside centers of Wheels together if desired. ❑❑

Work Boots

SIZES:
Small Sole is 3½" long.
Medium Sole is 4¼" long.
Large Sole is 5" long.

MATERIALS:
❏ Worsted yarn:
   42 yds. med. brown
   30 yds. beige
   5 yds. dk. brown
❏ F or G hook or hook needed
   to obtain gauge

GAUGES:
F hook, 9 sc = 2"; 9 sc rows = 2".
G hook, 4 sc = 1"; 4 sc rows = 1".

BASIC STITCHES:
Ch, sl st, sc, hdc, dc.

NOTES:
Do not join rnds unless otherwise stated.
For **Small,** use F hook and directions outside brackets [ ].
For **Medium,** use G hook and directions outside brackets [ ].
For **Large,** use G hook and directions inside brackets [ ].

SOLE
Rnd 1: With beige, ch 12 [14], sc in second ch from hook, sc in next 7 [9] chs, hdc in next ch, 2 hdc in next ch, 5 hdc in end ch; working in remaining lps on opposite side of starting ch, 2 hdc in next ch, hdc in next ch, sc in next 7 [9] chs, 2 sc in next ch.

Rnd 2: 2 sc in next st, sc in next 10 [12] sts, (2 sc in next st, sc in next st) 3 times, sc in next 9 [11] sts, 2 sc in next st, sc in next st.

Rnd 3: 2 sc in next st, sc in next 11 [13] sts, (2 sc in next st, sc in next st) 2 times, (sc in next st, 2 sc in next st) 2 times, sc in next 11 [13] sts, 2 sc in next st, sc in next st, join with sl st in next st, **turn.**

Rnd 4: For **Edge of Sole,** working in **back lps** only *(see Stitch Guide),* ch 1, sc in each st around, join with sl st in first sc. Fasten off. *(39 sc made)* [43 sc made]

SIDE
Rnd 1: With Edge of Sole facing you, working in remaining **front lps** of rnd 3, join med. brown with sc in first st after sl st of rnd 3, sc in each st around.

Rnd 2: Sc in each st around.

Rnd 3: Sc in next 13 [15] sts, (skip next st, sc in next 2 sts) 4 times, sc in next 14 [16] sts, join with sl st in next st. Fasten off.

INSTEP & TONGUE
Row 1: Skip first 11 [12] sts of rnd 3 on Side; working in **back lps** only, join med. brown with sl st in next st, ch 1, sc same st that sl st was worked in and next st tog, (sc next 2 sts tog) ♦ times, sl st in next st, turn.

Row 2: Skip sl st, sc in next st

(skip next st, sc in next st) 2 times, sl st in **back lp** of next st on Side, turn.

Row 3: Skip sl st, sc in next 3 sts, sl st in **back lp** of next st on Side, turn.

Row 4: Skip sl st, sc in next 3 sts, skip next st on Side, sl st in **back lp** of next st, turn.

Row 5: Skip sl st, sc in last 3 sts, turn.

Row 6: Ch 1, sc in first st, 2 sc in next st, sc in last st, turn.

Rows 7–13: Ch 1, sc in each st across, turn. At end of last row, fasten off.

TOP

Row 1: With toe of shoe pointing toward you, join med. brown with sc in **back lp** of same st that last st on row 1 of Instep was worked *(see illustration)*, sc in **both lps** of next 20 [24] sts, sc in **back lp** of same st that first st of row 1 of Instep was worked, turn.

JOIN

Row 2: Ch 1, skip first st, sc in next 19 [23] sts, skip next st, sc in last st, turn.

Row 3: Ch 1, skip first st, sc in next 17 [21] sts, skip next st, sc in last st, turn.

Row 4: Ch 1, skip first st, sc in next 15 [19] sts, skip next st, sc in last st, turn.

Rows 5–8: Ch 1, sc in each st across, turn. At end of last row, fasten off.

Row 9: Join beige with sc in first st, sc in each st across. Fasten off.

TRIM

With beige, using backstitch *(see illustration)*, embroider stitch-

BACKSTITCH

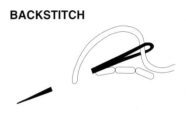

ing lines on sides and back of shoe *(see illustration)*.

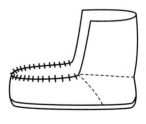

With beige, overcast *(see illustration)* **front lps** of rnd 3 on Side at base of Instep as shown in photo.

SHOESTRING

With dk. brown, ch 80. Fasten

off. Tie a knot at each end of Shoestring.

Lace Shoestring through edges of Top as shown in photo. Tie ends in a bow. ❏❏

OVERCAST

Track Shoes

SIZES:
Small Sole is 3½" long.
Medium Sole is 4¼" long.
Large Sole is 5" long.

MATERIALS:
❏ Worsted yarn:
  35 yds. white
  22 yds. blue
  34 yds. gold
❏ F or G hook or hook needed to obtain gauge

GAUGES:
F hook, 9 sc = 2"; 9 sc rows = 2".
G hook, 4 sc = 1"; 4 sc rows = 1".

BASIC STITCHES:
Ch, sl st, sc, hdc, dc.

NOTES:
Do not join rnds unless otherwise stated.
For **Small,** use F hook and directions outside brackets [ ].
For **Medium,** use G hook and directions outside brackets [ ].
For **Large,** use G hook and directions inside brackets [ ].

SOLE
Rnd 1: With gold, ch 12 [14], sc in second ch from hook, sc in next 7 [9] chs, hdc in next ch, 2 hdc in next ch, 5 hdc in end ch; working in remaining lps on opposite side of starting ch, 2 hdc in next ch, hdc in next ch, sc in next 7 [9] chs, 2 sc in next ch.

NOTE: For **3-dc cluster,** yo, insert hook in st, yo, pull through st, yo, pull through 2 lps on hook, (yo, insert hook in same st, yo, pull through st, yo, pull through 2 lps on hook) 2 times, yo and pull through all 4 lps on hook.

Rnd 2: 2 sc in first sc of last rnd, sc in next st, **3-dc cluster** (see Note) in next st, (sc in next 3 [4] sts, 3-dc cluster in next st) 2 times, 2 sc in next st, sc in next st, (sc, 3-dc cluster) in next st, sc in next st, 2 sc in next st, 3-dc cluster in next st, (sc in next 3 [4] sts, 3-dc cluster in next st) 2 times, sc in next st, 2 sc in next st, 3-dc cluster in next st.

Rnd 3: 2 sc in next st, sc in next 11 [13] sts, (2 sc in next st, sc in next st) 2 times, (sc in next st, 2 sc in next st) 2 times, sc in next 11 [13] sts, 2 sc in next st, sc in next st, join with sl st in next st.

Rnd 4: Working in **back lps**

only (see Stitch Guide), sc in next 15 [17] sts, hdc in next 2 sts, dc in next 4 sts, hdc in next 2 sts, sc in next 16 [18] sts, join with sl st in first sc. Fasten off. *(39 sts made)* [43 sts made]

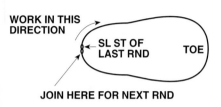

WORK IN THIS DIRECTION

SL ST OF LAST RND

TOE

JOIN HERE FOR NEXT RND

SIDE
Rnd 1: Working in **back lps** only, join blue with sc in st before sl st of last rnd, sc in next 15 [16] sts, skip next st, sc in next 6 sts, skip next st, sc in next 15 [18] sts. *(37 sc made)* [41 sc made]

Rnd 2: Sc in next 14 [16] sts, (skip next st, sc in next 2 sts) 3 times, skip next st, sc in 13 [15] sts. *(33 sc)* [37 sc]

Rnd 3: Sc in next 14 [16] sts, (sc next 2 sts tog) 3 times, sc in next 13 [15] sts, join with sl st in next st. Fasten off.

TAB AT HEEL OF SHOE
Working in **front lps** of rnd 4 on Sole in the center 5 sts at heel,

HEEL

JOIN

join gold with sl st in first of 5 sts, sc in next st, 3 hdc in next st, sc in next st, sl st in next st. Fasten off.

STOCKING INSTEP
Row 1: Working in **back lps** only of the center 4 sts at toe end of Shoe, join white with sl st in first st, ch 1, sc first st and st next tog, sc next 2 sts tog, turn. *(2 sc made)*

Rows 2–5: Ch 1, sc in each st across, turn. At end of last row, fasten off.

STOCKING
Rnd 1: Working in **back lps** only, join white with sc in st before sl st of rnd 3 on Side, sc in next 10 [12] sts, ch 1, sc in 2 sts at top of Instep, ch 1, sc in last 9 [11] sts of rnd 3.

Rnd 2: Sc in each sc around. *(22 sc)* [26 sc]

Rnd 3: Sc in each st around, join with sl st in first st.

Rnd 4: Ch 3, dc in each st around, join with sl st in top of ch-3.

Rnds 5–6: Ch 3, **dc front post** *(dc fp—see Stitch Guide)* around next st, *dc in next st, dc fp around next st; repeat from * around, join. For **Small and Medium** only, fasten off at end of rnd 6.

Rnd [7]: For **Large** only, ch 3, dc fp around next st, *dc in next st, dc fp around next st; repeat from * around, join. Fasten off.

Rnd 7 [8]: Join gold with sl st in same st as sl st of last rnd, ch 2, hdc fp around next st, *hdc in next st, hdc around post of next st; repeat from * around, join with sl st in top of ch-2. Fasten off.

Rnd 8 [9]: With white, repeat rnd 7 [8].

STRIPES ON SIDES

Working at middle on one side of shoe for first Stripe *(see photo)*, join gold with sl st in **front lp** of one st on rnd 4 of Sole, loosely ch 4, sl st at top edge of Side *(see illustration)*. Fasten off.

Skip one st and repeat for second Stripe.

Repeat Stripes on opposite side of shoe.

TOP PIECE

With blue, ch 15, dc in fourth ch from hook, dc in next 3 chs, 2 dc in next ch, 4 dc in next ch, 2 dc in next ch, dc in next 4 chs, (dc, hdc) in last ch. Leaving long end for tacking, fasten off.

SHOESTRING

With gold, ch 80. Fasten off.

Lace Shoestring through edges at center of Top Piece as shown in photo. Tie ends in a bow.

Tack outer edge of Top Piece over Instep of Stocking and top edge of Side *(see photo)*. ❏❏

Indian Moccasins

SIZES:

Small Sole is 3½" long.
Medium Sole is 4¼" long.
Large Sole is 5" long.

MATERIALS:

❏ 60 yds. gold worsted yarn
❏ F or G hook or hook needed to obtain gauge

GAUGES:

F hook, 9 sc = 2"; 9 sc rows = 2".
G hook, 4 sc = 1"; 4 sc rows = 1".

BASIC STITCHES:

Ch, sl st, sc, hdc.

NOTES:

Do not join rnds unless otherwise stated.

For **Small,** use F hook and directions outside brackets [ ].

For **Medium,** use G hook and directions outside brackets [ ].

For **Large,** use G hook and directions inside brackets [ ].

SOLE

Rnd 1: Ch 11 [13], 3 sc in second ch from hook, sc in next 8 [10] chs, 5 sc in end ch; working in remaining lps on opposite side of starting ch, sc in next 9 [11] chs.

Rnd 2: 2 sc in each of next 2 sts, sc in next 9 [11] sts, (2 sc in next st, sc in next st) 3 times, sc in next 8 [10] sts.

Rnd 3: 2 sc in next st, sc in next 2 sts, 2 sc in next st, sc in next 9 [11] sts, (2 sc in next st, sc in next 2 sts, 2 sc in next st) 2 times, sc in next 9 [11] sts, sc in next st.

Rnd 4: 2 sc in next st, sc in next 2 sts, 2 sc in next st, sc in next 11 [13] sts, (2 sc in next st, sc in next st) 2 times, sc in next 3 sts, (2 sc in next st, sc in next st) 2 times, sc in next 9 [11] sts.

Rnd 5: Sc in each st around.

Rnd 6: Sc in next 24 (26) sts, (skip next st, sc in next st) 3 times, sc in next 12 [14] sts, sc in next 2 sts.

Rnd 7: Sc in next 21 [23] sts, skip next st, sc in next 2 sts, skip next st, sc in next 14 [16] sts.

Rnd 8: Sc in next 18 [20] sts, (skip next st, sc in next 3 sts) 2 times, skip next st, sc in next 9 [11] sts.

Rnd 9: Sc in next 17 [19] sts, (skip next st, sc in next st) 2 times, sc in next st, (skip next st, sc in next st) 2 times, sc in next 8 [10] sts.

Rnd 10: Sc in next 16 [18] sts, (skip next st, sc in next st) 3 times, sc in next 8 [10] sts.

Rnd 11: Sc in next 14 [16] sts, (skip next st, sc in next st) 4 times, sc in next 22 [26] sts. *(This takes you to center front of the Moccasin.)*

Rnd 12: (Ch 1, skip next st, hdc in next 3 sts) 5 [6] times, ch 1, skip next st, sl st in next st, **turn.**

Row 13: *(This row forms the fringe);* skip first st, sc in next st, (ch 4, sl st in second ch from hook, sl st in next 2 chs, sc in **back lp**—*see Stitch Guide*—of next st on last rnd) 18 [21] times, sl st in next st, **turn.**

Row 14: Working in **remaining lps** of rnd 12, sc in each across to last st, sl st in last st. Fasten off.

TIE

Ch 65 [70]. Fasten off.

Thread Tie through spaces of rnd 12 under fringe. Tie ends in a bow. ❑❑

ISBN-13: 978-1-59635-146-2   ISBN-10: 1-59635-146-2

Chain—ch: Yo, pull through lp on hook.

Slip stitch—sl st: Insert hook in st, yo, pull through both lps on hook.

Single crochet—sc: Insert hook in st, yo, pull through st, yo, pull through both lps on hook.

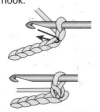

Front loop—front lp: Back loop—back lp:

Front Loop   Back Loop

Change colors: Drop first color; with second color, pull through last 2 lps of st.

Half double crochet— hdc: Yo, insert hook in st, yo, pull through st, yo, pull through all 3 lps on hook.

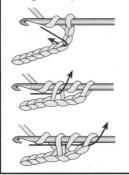

Double crochet—dc: Yo, insert hook in st, yo, pull through st, (yo, pull through 2 lps) 2 times.

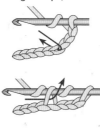

Treble crochet—tr: Yo 2 times, insert hook in st, yo, pull through st, (yo, pull through 2 lps) 3 times.

Double treble crochet— dtr: Yo 3 times, insert hook in st, yo, pull through st, (yo, pull through 2 lps) 4 times.

The patterns in this book are written using American crochet stitch terminology. For our international customers, hook sizes, stitches and yarn definitions should be converted as follows:

US	=	UK
sl st (slip stitch)	=	sc (single crochet)
sc (single crochet)	=	dc (double crochet)
hdc (half double crochet)	=	htr (half treble crochet)
dc (double crochet)	=	tr (treble crochet)
tr (treble crochet)	=	dtr (double treble crochet)
dtr (double treble crochet)	=	ttr (triple treble crochet)
skip	=	miss

THREAD/YARNS

Bedspread Weight	=	No. 10 Cotton or Virtuoso
Sport Weight	=	4 Ply or thin DK
Worsted Weight	=	Thick DK or Aran

MEASUREMENTS

1"	=	2.54 cm
1 yd.	=	.9144 m
1 oz.	=	28.35 g

But, as with all patterns, test your gauge (tension) to be sure.

CROCHET HOOKS

Metric	US	Metric	US
.60mm	14	3.00mm	D/3
.75mm	12	3.50mm	E/4
1.00mm	10	4.00mm	F/5
1.50mm	6	4.50mm	G/6
1.75mm	5	5.00mm	H/8
2.00mm	B/1	5.50mm	I/9
2.50mm	C/2	6.00mm	J/10